Exploring Physical Science

Exploring

CHEMICAL REACTIONS

Nigel Saunders

rosen publishing's
rosen central

New York

Published in 2008 by The Rosen Publishing Group, Inc.
29 East 21st Street, New York, NY 10010

First Edition

Cover: Charles D. Winters/Science Photo library; p. 4: istockphoto.com; p. 5: G. K. Hart/
Vikki Hart/Getty Images; p. 7: Andy Green/istockphoto.com; p. 11: Hulton Archive/Getty
Images; p. 12: Andrew Lambert/LGPL/Alamy; p. 13: Martin Bond/Science Photo Library;
p. 14: James Holmes/Zedcar/Science Photo Library; p. 15: Phil Degginger/Getty Images; p. 16:
Gail Schumway/Getty Images; p. 17: Patrik Giardino/Getty Images; p. 18: Bruce Forster/Getty
Images; p. 21: E. R. Degginger/Science Photo Library; p. 22: Martina Berg/istockphoto.com;
p. 23: Ron Smith/istockphoto.com; p. 25: Andrew Lambert/LGPL/Alamy; p. 26: Cezar
Serbanescu/istockphoto.com; p. 27: Rob Bowden/EASI-Images/cfwimages.com; p. 29:
Andrew Lambert Photography/Science Photo Library; p. 31: Mark Pruitt/istockphoto.com;
p. 33: Mansell/Time Life Pictures/Getty Images; p. 34: Charles D. Winters/Science Photo
library; p. 36: Malcolm Romain/istockphoto.com; p. 37: Chris Fairclough/cfwimages.com;
p. 40: Edward Parker/EASI-Images/cfwimages.com; p. 41: Vera Bogaerts/istockphoto.com;
p. 43: istockphoto.com; p. 45: Daimler Chrysler, Project: Fuel cell buses.

Library of Congress Cataloging-in-Publication Data

Saunders, N. (Nigel)
  Chemical reactions / Nigel Saunders.
      p. cm. -- (Exploring Physical Science)
  Includes index.
  ISBN-13: 978-1-4042-3751-3 (library binding)
  ISBN-10: 1-4042-3751-8 (library binding)
  1. Chemical reactions--Juvenile literature. 1. Title.
  QD501.S2518 2007
  541'.39--dc22

                                        2006039146

Manufactured in China

Contents

CHAPTER I

What are chemical reactions?

Which of the following do you think involves chemical reactions: an egg frying; glue setting; a banana ripening; a car engine running; or a bicycle chain turning rusty? In fact, they all involve chemical reactions. In each case, substances join together in different ways to make new substances, and this is what chemistry is all about.

Chemical reactions are everywhere

Chemical reactions are happening around you all the time. They are even happening inside you. Thanks to chemical reactions, you can move, grow, and do lots of other things.

Even a sheep is a chemist. The grass it eats is broken down into tiny pieces called **molecules**. The sheep's **cells** use these for energy. They also join molecules together in different ways to make new substances, letting the sheep grow and repair its body. These things all need chemical reactions.

When a sheep grazes on grass, chemical reactions in its body turn the grass into energy and body tissue.

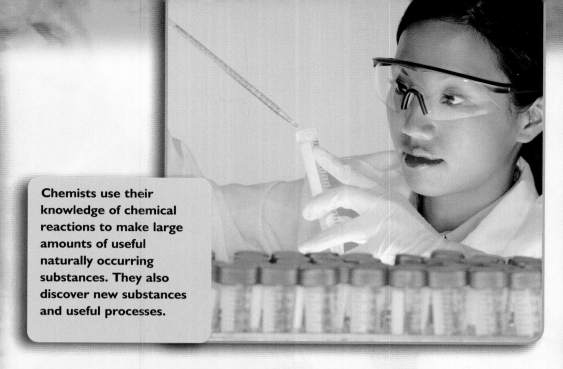

Chemists use their knowledge of chemical reactions to make large amounts of useful naturally occurring substances. They also discover new substances and useful processes.

In this book, you will find out all about chemical reactions, what they are, what they do, different types of chemical reaction, and how you can tell that one is happening.

 THE MOST REACTIVE ELEMENTS

The most **reactive** metal you are likely to see at school is potassium. Only experienced chemists are allowed to use it, because it reacts dangerously with water. They have to use a piece no bigger than a grain of rice in their experiments, and protect everyone with safety glasses and a safety screen. But the most reactive **element** of all is fluorine.

Fluorine reacts with water and moisture in the air to make hydrofluoric acid. This is so strong that it even attacks glass. Fluorine is so dangerous that it killed or injured the chemists who first tried to prepare it. Sir Humphry Davy, the English chemist who discovered potassium in 1807, was poisoned by fluorine, but luckily he recovered. Several other chemists were later poisoned by it. Two died and another narrowly avoided being blown up. Fluorine was at last safely prepared in 1886 by the French chemist, Henri Moisson.

Chemical changes and physical changes

There are two main types of change that can happen to a substance. Chemical changes happen because of chemical reactions, but how can you tell them from simple physical changes?

Change or no change?

Physical changes are very common. Whenever you bend, break, or cut something, you cause a physical change. But if you cut a piece of paper it is still paper. It hasn't changed into a new substance. You can also cause a physical change when you heat or cool something. If you freeze some water, it is still water, just solid rather than liquid.

The key feature of any chemical reaction is that one or more new substances are made when it happens. This often means that you see a change in color or a gas being made. For example, food is cooked because of chemical reactions. The substances in the raw ingredients change into new and different substances when they are heated in a pan or the oven. This means that a chemical reaction has taken place. Instead, physical changes do not produce any new substances.

Irreversible or reversible?

When you make a piece of toast, the heat from the toaster causes chemical reactions in the bread and it gradually turns crisp and brown. Once this has happened, you cannot change the toast back into a slice of bread again. This is because chemical reactions usually cause permanent changes that are difficult to reverse.

 THE PHILOSOPHER'S STONE

Before chemical reactions were understood properly, an early kind of science called **alchemy** was followed by people called alchemists. They were interested in many different things, but they are probably most famous for trying to convert lead into gold. To do this, they conducted many experiments in an attempt to find a substance that they called the Philosopher's Stone. The alchemists believed that this was vital for turning lead into gold. We now know that it is impossible to convert lead into gold using chemical reactions.

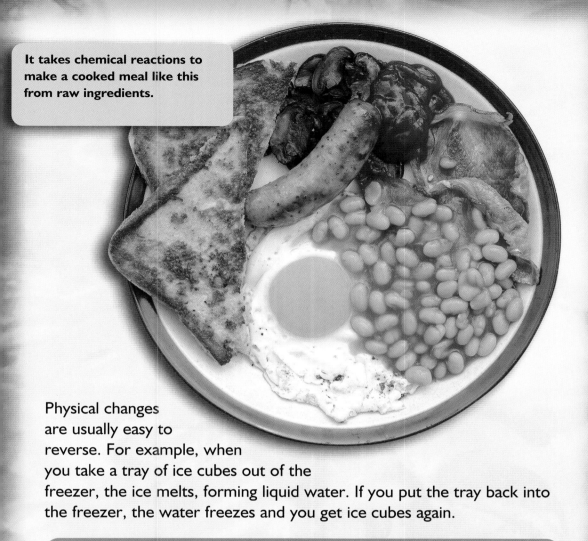

It takes chemical reactions to make a cooked meal like this from raw ingredients.

Physical changes are usually easy to reverse. For example, when you take a tray of ice cubes out of the freezer, the ice melts, forming liquid water. If you put the tray back into the freezer, the water freezes and you get ice cubes again.

 AMAZING FACTS

The Mpemba Effect

Warm water can freeze faster than cold water, unless there is a big difference in starting temperatures. It might seem impossible, but it's true. It is called **The Mpemba Effect**, after the school student in Tanzania who discovered it in 1963. The reasons why are very complex. When a container of water is put in the freezer, the heat it has is transferred more quickly if the water is warm than if it is cold.

CHAPTER 2

Describing chemical reactions

Imagine that you were asked to get a bottle of water. It would probably be an easy thing to do, because you already know what water looks like. But would you be so sure what to get if someone asked you for water in another language? Things get more difficult with substances like sodium chloride (also known as table salt), and even more difficult with substances with complex names like trichloromethane. Problems like these face chemists all the time, so to make everything easier, they use chemical symbols.

Chemical symbols

Elements are substances that are made of only one type of **atom**, such as hydrogen and oxygen. You cannot change an element into a different element using chemical reactions, and just over a hundred different elements are known. Every element has its own chemical symbol, made from one or two letters. The first letter is always a capital letter and the other letter is always lowercase. So mercury is always written as **Hg** and not "HG," "hG," or "hg."

 COMMON CHEMICAL SYMBOLS

Many elements have a symbol that begins with the first letter of their English name, but others do not. This is because their symbol comes from the element's name in a different language. For example, "Fe" comes from "ferrum," which is Latin for iron; and "Na" comes from "natrium," which is Latin for salt.

element	symbol
carbon	C
chlorine	Cl
hydrogen	H
iron	Fe
oxygen	O
sodium	Na

Chemical formulae

A substance made from two or more atoms joined together is given a chemical formula. The formula for oxygen gas is O_2, which tells us that it is made from two oxygen atoms joined together. The formula for water is H_2O. This means that water is made from two hydrogen atoms and one oxygen atom joined together.

AMAZING FACTS

Growing numbers

The American Chemical Society keeps a database of all the different substances discovered or made by scientists. The database contains about 29 million different substances, and around 4,000 new chemicals are added to it every day.

The formula for sodium chloride is NaCl. You can tell that sodium chloride contains only two elements, even though its formula has four letters, because there are only two capital letters. Trichloromethane has a complex name but a fairly simple formula, $CHCl_3$. This tells you that it is made from one carbon atom, one hydrogen atom, and three chlorine atoms. The great thing about chemical symbols and formulae is that they are the same everywhere in the world.

he periodic table
ontains the symbols
f all the elements.
he elements are
rranged so that the
toms get heavier as
ou go from left to
ght. Elements with
milar properties
re in vertical
olumns called
roups. Elements 57-
I and 89-103 are so
milar to each other,
ey are put in a
eparate block
ogether at
he bottom.

| | | | | | | | | | | | | | | | | | H 1 | | | | | | | | | | | | | | | | | | He 2 |

Li 3	Be 4											B 5	C 6	N 7	O 8	F 9	Ne 10
Na 11	Mg 12											Al 13	Si 14	P 15	S 16	Cl 17	Ar 18
K 19	Ca 20	Sc 21	Ti 22	V 23	Cr 24	Mn 25	Fe 26	Co 27	Ni 28	Cu 29	Zn 30	Ga 31	Ge 32	As 33	Se 34	Br 35	Kr 36
Rb 37	Sr 38	Y 39	Zr 40	Nb 41	Mo 42	Tc 43	Ru 44	Rh 45	Pd 46	Ag 47	Cd 48	In 49	Sn 50	Sb 51	Te 52	I 53	Xe 54
Cs 55	Ba 56	57–71	Hf 72	Ta 73	W 74	Re 75	Os 76	Ir 77	Pt 78	Au 79	Hg 80	Tl 81	Pb 82	Bi 83	Po 84	At 85	Rn 86
Fr 87	Ra 88	89–103	Rf 104	Db 105	Sg 106	Bh 107	Hs 108	Mt 109	Ds 110	Rg 111							

La 57	Ce 58	Pr 59	Nd 60	Pm 61	Sm 62	Eu 63	Gd 64	Tb 65	Dy 66	Ho 67	Er 68	Tm 69	Yb 70	Lu 71
Ac 89	Th 90	Pa 91	U 92	Np 93	Pu 94	Am 95	Cm 96	Bk 97	Cf 98	Es 99	Fm 100	Md 101	No 102	Lr 103

Metals   Metalloids   Non−metals

Chemical equations

If you watch a chemical reaction, such as sodium metal reacting with chlorine gas, you can describe the reaction by saying things like "it makes a flame," "it makes a lot of heat," and so on. But you also need to be able to say what chemicals are reacting and what chemicals are being made in the reaction. To do this, you use chemical equations.

Word equations

A **word equation** gives the names of all the substances involved in a chemical reaction. The substances that react together are called the **reactants**. The substances that are made in the reaction are called the **products**. In general, you can say:

reactants ➜ products

The arrow means "make," so you can say that the reactants make the products. If there is more than one reactant or product, you separate them using a plus sign. This is the word equation for sodium and chlorine reacting:

sodium + chlorine ➜ sodium chloride

It tells you that sodium and chlorine are the reactants, and that they react together to make sodium chloride, which is the product.

 AMAZING FACTS

A tongue twister

The big number in front of a chemical formula in a symbol equation is called the **stoichiometric coefficient** (pronounced "stoy-key-oh-metric co-eh-fish-ent"). Impress your friends with that one!

GREAT SCIENTISTS

Antoine Lavoisier

In the eighteenth century, Antoine Lavoisier, a French chemist, discovered that the total mass of substances always stays the same in a chemical reaction. If you weigh all the chemicals at the start of the reaction, and then weigh the chemicals at the end, you will find that their total weight has remained the same. This is called the **Law of Conservation of Mass**.

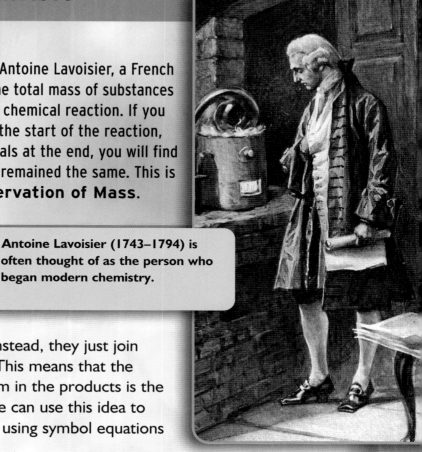

Antoine Lavoisier (1743–1794) is often thought of as the person who began modern chemistry.

Nothing lost, nothing gained

In a chemical reaction none of the **atoms** are lost, and none are gained. Instead, they just join together in different ways. This means that the number of each type of atom in the products is the same as in the reactants. We can use this idea to describe chemical reactions using symbol equations instead of word equations.

$$2H_2 + O_2 \rightarrow 2H_2O$$

This equation tells you that hydrogen and oxygen react together to make water. The big numbers next to H_2 and H_2O are different from the numbers inside each formula—they tell you that you need two **molecules** of hydrogen and two molecules of water to balance the equation. A symbol equation is balanced when the number of each type of atom is the same on both sides of the arrow. In this case, the big "two" in front of the H_2O means we have two times two hydrogen atoms, and two times one oxygen atom. There are four hydrogen atoms on each side, and two oxygen atoms on each side, so the equation is balanced. Just like chemical symbols and formulae, symbol equations are the same everywhere.

CHAPTER 3

Chemistry all around you

Your body carries out millions of chemical reactions all the time, even when you are just reading this book. You probably don't even notice them. But you would be in trouble if they stopped, because living things die if the chemical reactions in their **cells** stop.

Respiration

The food you eat is needed to supply your body with energy, and to let it grow and repair itself. Chemical reactions allow these things to happen. **Respiration** is the chemical reaction that releases energy from food, such as glucose, which is a type of sugar. You need oxygen for respiration to happen, which is why you breathe air into your lungs. The products of respiration are carbon dioxide and water. When you breathe out again, these waste substances go out of your lungs and into the air. You can see the water vapor when you breathe out on a cold day. These are the equations for respiration:

glucose + oxygen → carbon dioxide + water

$$C_6H_{12}O_6 + 6O_2 \rightarrow 6CO_2 + 6H_2O$$

Limewater turns cloudy white in the presence of carbon dioxide.

 YOUR OWN BREATH

Normal air contains about 0.038 percent carbon dioxide, but the air we breathe out contains about 4.5 percent carbon dioxide. We can detect this using limewater, which turns cloudy white when we breathe into it.

GREAT EXPERIMENTS

Van Helmont's willow tree

In the seventeenth century, Jan Baptista van Helmont conducted an experiment that took five years to complete. He wanted to prove that plants grow from water alone. He planted a willow tree in a container of dry soil. For the next five years, he watered the tree and watched it grow. At the end of the experiment, the soil weighed the same after drying it, but the tree weighed 164 lbs (74.4 kg) more than at the start. Van Helmont thought this proved the tree grew from the water alone, but we now know he was wrong: carbon dioxide from the air is also needed.

Respiration happens all the time in our cells. It releases thermal energy, which is why we usually feel warmer to touch than the objects around us.

Willow grows very quickly, and today its wood is used for fuel.

Photosynthesis

Plants are able to make their own food using a chemical reaction called **photosynthesis**. Plant cells have **chloroplasts** in them, where carbon dioxide from the air can react with water from the soil to make glucose and oxygen. Light energy is needed to get this reaction to work, and plants usually get this from sunlight. Here are the equations for photosynthesis:

carbon dioxide + water → glucose + oxygen

$$6CO_2 + 6H_2O \rightarrow C_6H_{12}O_6 + 6O_2$$

13

It's a material world

Take a look around you. Most of the substances you see will be artificial, which means that they have been made by people using chemical reactions. Even most of the natural substances, such as wood, have been formed by chemical reactions.

Paper

Paper is made from wood, but the wood must be processed before it can be used. It is chopped into pieces and boiled with sodium **hydroxide** and other chemicals. This breaks the wood down, so that the fibers can be separated. These are bleached to make them white and mixed with water to make a sloppy mixture. This is spread out, pressed flat, and dried to make paper. Without those chemical reactions, you would be writing on thin pieces of wood instead of paper.

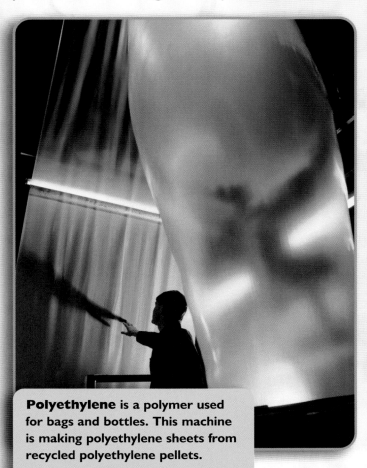

Polyethylene is a polymer used for bags and bottles. This machine is making polyethylene sheets from recycled polyethylene pellets.

Polymers

Plastics are very useful materials. For example, polypropene is used to make carpets and crates, and polystyrene is used to make lightweight packaging and disposable cups. Plastics consist of long **molecules** called **polymers**. These are made from thousands of small molecules, called **monomers,** which join end to end because of chemical reactions.

Metals

Some metals are **unreactive** and do not easily react with other substances. This means that when they are found in nature they do not have to be separated from other substances. They are not chemically joined to other **elements**. These metals are usually rare and expensive substances such as gold and platinum.

Most metals in nature are found already chemically joined with other elements such as oxygen. Rocks that contain useful amounts of metal **compounds** are called **ores**. We need to use chemical reactions to separate a metal from the other elements in its ore so that we can use it. For example, iron is extracted from iron ore, which is usually the ore called iron **oxide**. The iron ore is heated with carbon or carbon monoxide to separate the iron.

Iron is extracted from iron ore in a huge reaction container called a **blast furnace**.

NAPOLEON'S PLATES

Very **reactive** metals, such as aluminum, join tightly with other elements, so they are difficult to extract. You probably take aluminum foil and cans for granted. But in the nineteenth century, aluminum was so difficult to extract that it cost more than gold, and Napoleon III of France liked to impress his guests with aluminum plates. Things changed in 1886 when the Hall-Héroult process was invented. It used electricity to extract aluminum more easily and cheaply. The process is still used today.

Exothermic reactions

Chemical reactions make new substances and they also involve energy changes. Reactions that give off energy are called **exothermic reactions**.

Exothermic reactions are the most common type of chemical reaction. They can transfer energy in all kinds of different forms. For example, fires give out heat and light energy as the fuel reacts with oxygen in the air; explosions give out sound energy and **kinetic energy** as hot gases expand outward rapidly; and batteries give out electrical energy.

However, energy is usually transferred as heat energy, so one way to tell if a chemical reaction is happening is to use a thermometer. If the temperature increases during a chemical reaction, you know that it is an exothermic reaction. **Respiration** is an exothermic reaction.

LIGHT STICKS AND FIREFLIES

Light sticks are transparent plastic tubes with two compartments, each containing a different mix of chemicals. When the light stick is bent, the inner compartment breaks allowing all the chemicals to mix. The exothermic chemical reaction between them releases light energy, often for several hours. Fireflies are insects that glow or flash at night, but instead of plastic compartments, they contain a chemical called luciferin that gives off light when it is changed by an **enzyme** called luciferase.

Fireflies give off light because of exothermic chemical reactions that involve luciferin and luciferase.

Endothermic reactions

Exothermic reactions transfer energy to the surroundings, and **endothermic reactions** transfer energy from the surroundings. This often means that the temperature of the reaction mixture goes down as heat energy is drawn away from the test tube or beaker. For example, when ammonium nitrate dissolves in water, the temperature drops several degrees. This kind of reaction is useful for instant cold packs to treat sprains or to keep picnic food chilled.

Endothermic reactions only happen while there is a supply of energy, usually heat energy. **Photosynthesis**, used by plants to make their own food, is an endothermic reaction that needs a supply of light energy. Copper carbonate is a green solid that breaks down when heated, to form black copper **oxide** and carbon dioxide. This kind of chemical reaction is called a thermal decomposition reaction: "thermal," because heat is needed, and "decomposition," because the chemical breaks down or decomposes.

 RECHARGEABLE BATTERIES

Batteries give out electrical energy because of exothermic chemical reactions between the chemicals inside them. They go flat when the supply of **reactants** has been used up and the reactions stop. Rechargeable batteries are different from normal batteries. They can be charged up again by transferring electricity back into them, which reverses the chemical reactions.

Step back!

Some chemical reactions start on their own as soon as the **reactants** are mixed. Others need a burst of energy to get them going, usually in the form of heat energy.

Need a kick-start?

Iron reacts with water and oxygen from the air to form rust without needing a boost of energy. However, most reactions need some energy to get going. Burning, for example, only happens when fuel reaches a high enough temperature. Explosives need energy to make them explode. This is usually electrical energy or heat energy, but nitroglycerine will explode just by knocking it.

Fast or slow?

Some chemical reactions are slow, but others are very fast. Rusting is a slow reaction. Although rust can appear within days on an iron or steel object, it may be many years before all the metal has rusted. It takes several hours for paint to dry and harden completely, but an egg cooks in minutes. **Neutralization**, burning, and explosions are all fast reactions.

The chemical reactions in demolition explosives are started using electrical energy.

In the blink of an eye

Rhodopsin is one of the light-sensitive proteins in the eye that lets us see. When light hits it, rhodopsin changes in one of the fastest chemical reactions known. The reaction takes just 200 millionths of a billionth of a second to happen.

The speed of a chemical reaction can be increased by heating up the reactants, which is why you may use a Bunsen burner in school experiments. It is also why food rots more quickly in hot weather. Refrigerators keep food fresh for longer, because chemical reactions in the food happen more slowly in the cold.

Chemical hazards

Any substance could be dangerous if it is not handled correctly. Hazard labels are put on bottles and other containers of chemicals to warn you of the dangers inside. You should always treat unknown chemicals as dangerous, just to be on the safe side.

 GREAT SCIENTISTS

Henry Talbot

The Englishman, William Henry Fox Talbot, is often called the father of modern photography. His method was the first to use light-sensitive paper, fixing, and printing. He treated the paper with silver chloride, a salt that breaks down when light energy reaches it. Photographs were taken by exposing the paper to light from the scene. Talbot patented his process in 1841, and although it has been improved greatly since then, modern photographic film still uses silver salts.

CHAPTER 4

Acids and bases

You may have come across strong **acids** like hydrochloric acid and sulfuric acid in the school laboratory, but did you know that the acid in your stomach is hydrochloric acid? Too much stomach acid causes painful indigestion, and if you have ever vomited, you will know how much it stings your throat. There are many weak acids, too, and you certainly have swallowed some of them, because they are found in foods and drinks.

What are acids like?

Acids have some properties in common. They have a sour taste (but never taste anything in a laboratory), they sting your skin, and they react with metals. Strong acids are very dangerous, but they might be diluted with water to make them safer to use. Weak acids are less dangerous but must still be handled carefully.

Car batteries and pickling

Cars and other vehicles use a type of rechargeable battery called a **lead-acid battery**. The biggest single use of lead is in these heavy batteries, which are used to work the starter motor of an engine, lights, and other equipment. The acid used is concentrated sulfuric acid.

 AMAZING FACTS

Edible cleaning fluid

If you want to clean an old coin, just cover it in ketchup for a few minutes. Ketchup contains acetic acid, which is found in vinegar, too. Acetic acid gives foods a sharp taste. It reacts with the oxides on the surface of the coin and removes them, leaving a nice shiny coin behind—once you've washed the ketchup off, of course.

DANGER—CORROSIVE!

Acids are **corrosive** chemicals. This means that they will react with materials, such as metals, and damage them. They also react with living tissues, such as skin and eyes, damaging them, too. If you handle a corrosive substance, you should wear gloves and eye protection, such as goggles or a face shield. Hazard labels on bottles and other containers warn you if the substance inside is corrosive.

Hydrochloric acid is used to pickle iron and steel. This doesn't mean preserving it for later, but instead, it means cleaning the surface of the metal before painting. The acid reacts with iron **oxide** on the surface, forming iron chloride. This dissolves in the acid and leaves the surface free of any iron oxide that could stop the paint from sticking properly.

Acids in food and drink

Many different weak acids are found in foods and drinks. Vitamin C, found in citrus fruit and green vegetables, is needed to keep the body healthy. It is ascorbic acid. Tea contains tannic acid, grapes contain tartaric acid, and yogurt contains lactic acid. Carbonated drinks contain carbonic acid, and cola drinks also contain phosphoric acid (which is also used as rust remover!).

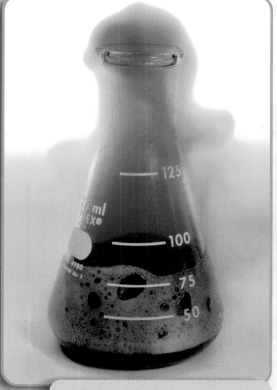

Copper does not react with most acids, but it will react rapidly with concentrated nitric acid. The brown fumes are poisonous nitrogen dioxide.

Chamomile flowers contain alkalis, and are used to make herbal tea to help indigestion. The alkali in the flowers neutralizes the acid in the stomach.

What are bases?

Bases are substances that can react with **acids** and **neutralize** them. Ammonia, metal **oxides**, metal **hydroxides,** and metal **carbonates** are all capable of neutralizing acids, so they are bases.

Bases and alkalis

Most bases are **insoluble**, so they cannot dissolve in water. The bases that are **soluble** are given an extra name. They are called **alkalis**. An alkali is a base that can dissolve in water. Just like any other base, alkalis can neutralize acids. Alkalis are **corrosive**, and they will damage living tissue and materials.

Alkalis have a bitter taste (never taste anything in a laboratory) and they feel soapy. Strong alkalis, like sodium hydroxide, are very dangerous, but they can be diluted with water to make them safer to use. Weak alkalis, like sodium hydrogen carbonate (known around the house as **baking soda**) and ammonia, are less dangerous, but they must still be handled carefully.

 SOAP

It is important to keep yourself clean. Apart from smelling better, hygiene is important to avoid spreading harmful disease-causing **microbes**. Soap has been used for hundreds of years and is made by heating an alkali, usually potassium hydroxide, with oil. The oil used to come from animal fats, but nowadays, it is likely to be a vegetable oil, such as olive oil.

ARABIC NAMES

The word **alkali** comes from the Arabic "al-qali," which means "the ashes." This is because when plants are burned, their ashes contain bases that dissolve in water to form an alkaline solution. Potassium, an alkali metal, gets it name from "potash," meaning "ashes from the pot."

Bases around the home

If you spill greasy food on your shirt, it is difficult to remove the stain. This is because oils and fats do not dissolve in water. Alkalis react with oils and fats to make products that do dissolve in water. It would be a bad idea to use an alkali to clean your clothes, because it is corrosive and will damage the fibers. Detergents are a better choice for that job, but alkalis are ideal if the grease is in the kitchen, bathroom, or you have a dirty drain.

Household cleaners contain alkalis, such as ammonia, sodium hydroxide, and potassium hydroxide. You have to be careful to wear gloves when you use them, and you must not use them on aluminum. This is because the alkali reacts with the protective layer of aluminum oxide and corrodes the aluminum underneath.

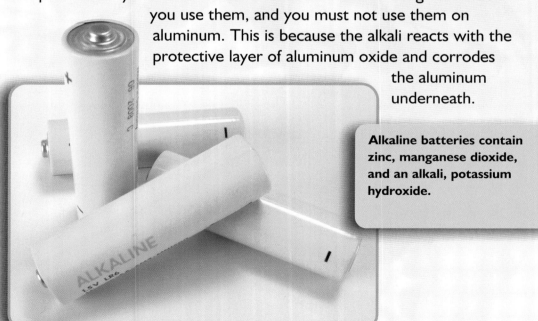

Alkaline batteries contain zinc, manganese dioxide, and an alkali, potassium hydroxide.

Neutralization

When **acids** and **bases** react together, they make neutral solutions. Chemical reactions like these are called **neutralization** reactions. You can check whether a solution is acidic, neutral, or **alkaline** using indicators.

Indicators

Indicators are chemicals that have different colors depending on whether they are in an acidic or alkaline solution. One common indicator is called **litmus**. People sometimes talk about giving something the "litmus test" if they want to find out what it is like. There are two types of litmus paper: red litmus and blue litmus. If you add a drop of liquid to the paper, the color may change. The table shows you the color changes for litmus paper.

	INDICATOR PAPER	
Solution tested	RED LITMUS	BLUE LITMUS
Acidic	Stays red	Turns red
Neutral	Stays red	Stays blue
Alkaline	Turns blue	Stays blue

Litmus paper is easy to use, but it only tells you if something is acidic, neutral, or alkaline, not how strongly acidic or alkaline it is. For this, you need to use a special combination of indicators called a universal indicator.

The color changes for litmus paper. You get the same color changes for litmus solution, except it turns purple in neutral solutions.

A GEOLOGIST'S TEST

Geologists are scientists who study rocks. They need to be able to identify different rocks. Limestone, chalk, and marble are three rocks made from calcium **carbonate**. To see if a rock contains calcium carbonate, the geologist adds a few drops of hydrochloric acid. Neutralization reactions involving carbonates produce carbon dioxide gas. This causes the rock to fizz when the acid touches it.

THE pH SCALE

The **pH** scale lets you measure how strong or weak an acid or alkali is. It runs from pH 0, which means strongly acidic, to pH 14, which means strongly alkaline. Neutral solutions are pH 7 exactly. Have a look at the shampoo and liquid soap bottles at home, as well as bottles of mineral water. They may say what pH level the product inside has.

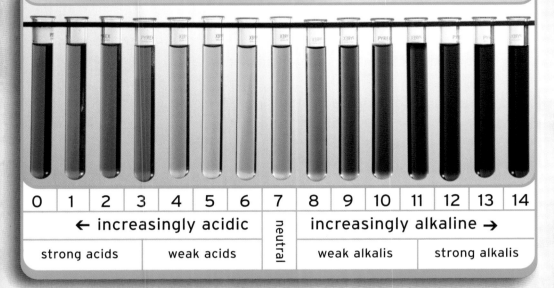

0	1	2	3	4	5	6	7	8	9	10	11	12	13	14

← increasingly acidic | neutral | increasingly alkaline →

| strong acids | weak acids | | weak alkalis | strong alkalis |

Common neutralization reactions

Neutralization reactions happen between an acid and a base, forming a neutral solution. These reactions are very useful, from treating indigestion to improving a farmer's crop. Wasp stings are alkaline and can be helped using vinegar, which is acidic.

Stomach acid is hydrochloric acid. Indigestion happens when too much of this is made. Indigestion remedies contain weak bases that neutralize the extra acid, making you feel better. Antacid tablets contain bases like sodium carbonate, and Milk of Magnesia is a thick white or pink medicine containing magnesium **hydroxide**.

It is difficult for most crops to grow well in acidic soil, so farmers spread powdered limestone (calcium carbonate) or lime (calcium **oxide**) over their fields. These bases neutralize the acids in the soil. Powdered limestone is also used to treat lakes that have become too acidic due to pollution.

Salts

Neutralization reactions between **acids** and **bases** always produce salts. You might think of the salt you put on your food, but that is sodium chloride. There are many different kinds of salts, which can be used for anything from fertilizers to fireworks.

Naming salts

The name of a salt comes from the base used and the acid it was reacted with. The first part of the name comes from the metal in the base. So sodium **hydroxide** can make salts whose names begin with "sodium," and copper **oxide** can make salts whose names begin with "copper".

The second part of the name comes from the acid used. So if sodium hydroxide reacts with hydrochloric acid, you get sodium chloride. Water is also made. Here are the equations for the reaction:

sodium hydroxide + hydrochloric acid → sodium chloride + water
$NaOH + HCl → NaCl + H_2O$

This is not how sodium chloride is made for use as table salt. It is difficult to add exactly the right amounts of acid and **alkali** to make sure that the final solution is exactly neutral. Table salt is obtained by purifying salt from salt mines or by evaporating seawater.

Sodium chloride is a salt that forms beautiful cubic crystals.

AMMONIUM SALTS

Ammonia is a weak alkali that does not contain any metal. It makes salts whose names begin with "ammonium." For example, ammonium phosphate fertilizer is made by reacting ammonia and phosphoric acid together.

AMAZING FACTS

Salts in fireworks

Oxidizers are substances that provide oxygen to make fuels burn quickly. Fireworks contain salts like potassium nitrate and potassium chlorate as oxidizers. Without them, the fuel in fireworks would burn too slowly to be very exciting. Fireworks also contain salts that give off colored flames in the heat. For example, copper chloride produces blue light, and barium chloride produces green.

Salts everywhere

Common table salt is sodium chloride. It is used to flavor food, though too much in your diet can cause high blood pressure. Very pure sodium chloride is also used as dishwasher salt. This keeps the built-in water softener working and stops the plates from getting white deposits on them.

Fireworks contain different salts to help them explode into many colors.

Plants use minerals from the soil as they grow. Nitrogen, phosphorus, and potassium are particularly important to plants, and fertilizers are used to provide enough for healthy plant growth. Salts, such as ammonium phosphate, potassium sulphate, and ammonium nitrate, are used in many fertilizers.

CHAPTER 5

Metals and reactions

Pieces of metal usually just get very hot if you put them in a flame, but if you look carefully, you will see signs of a chemical reaction happening. You can even get some metals to burn.

Oxidation

The air around us is a mix of gases, but just two of them account for 99 percent of it. Nitrogen forms 78 percent of the air and is fairly **unreactive**. Oxygen forms 21 percent of air and is the gas that other substances react with when they burn.

Oxidation is the chemical reaction when anything reacts with oxygen. Burning is an example of an oxidation reaction, and so is rusting. Most metals can **oxidize** in air, especially when they are very hot or powdered.

Reactive metals

Some metals are very reactive. They easily take part in chemical reactions with other substances, including oxygen in the air. Magnesium is a very **reactive** metal. Magnesium ribbon burns with a dazzling white flame if it is heated in a fire. The light is so bright that magnesium powder was used in flash photography in the early twentieth century.

 ALUMINUM VERSUS IRON

Aluminum is more reactive than iron, but iron rusts and aluminum does not. Rusting happens when iron reacts with air and water. But the surface of aluminum is naturally protected by an invisible thin layer of aluminum oxide. This layer sticks tightly to the aluminum and does not flake off. It protects the metal underneath from reacting with air and water.

SPARKLERS

Sparklers are familiar hand-held fireworks that make a brilliant shower of sparks. They have a mixture of chemicals attached to one end of a metal stick. The mixture contains a fuel, such as sugar, an **"oxidizer"** that speeds up the rate of burning, and powdered metal. The powdered metal is usually iron, aluminum, or magnesium. When the fuel is ignited, it makes enough heat to shoot out white-hot metal, which often burns in the air.

Unreactive metals

Gold and platinum do not react with oxygen at all, even if they are heated very strongly. Some other metals, such as copper, are a little more reactive. They react with oxygen if they are heated strongly, and turn black as a layer of their **oxide** forms. Silver does not react with pure air, but its surface turns black after awhile. This is because air usually contains small amounts of sulfur **compounds**. These react with the surface of the silver to form black silver sulfide, which is why silver needs to be polished every so often.

If it is heated, copper reacts with oxygen in the air to form black copper oxide.

Reactions of metals with water

You would probably be surprised if you dropped a piece of metal into water and saw it float, fizz, and then disappear. But that is just what some metals do.

Potassium is an unusual metal, because it actually floats on water instead of sinking. You might think that this would make it ideal for building ships. Unfortunately, potassium is very **reactive**. In fact, potassium bursts into flames as soon as it touches water. It crackles and fizzes, and gives off showers of sparks before finally exploding with a pop.

Potassium is not the only metal that reacts violently with water. It is one of a group of metals called the **alkali metals** that have similar chemical reactions. Lithium and sodium are less reactive than potassium, but rubidium and caesium are even more reactive.

Hydroxides and hydrogen

When any metal reacts with water, the chemical reaction makes a metal **hydroxide** and hydrogen gas. Here are the equations for the reaction between potassium and water:

potassium + water ➔ potassium hydroxide + hydrogen
$$2K + 2H_2O \rightarrow 2KOH + H_2$$

AMAZING FACTS

Plumbers

Lead does not react with water, so it was used since Roman times to make water pipes. The Latin word for lead is "plumbum," and this is where we get its chemical symbol (Pb) from, and why people who work with water pipes are called "plumbers." Over a period of time, lead becomes poisonous, so nowadays plumbers use copper or plastic pipes instead.

Potassium hydroxide is an **alkali**, which is why potassium is called an alkali metal. Hydrogen gas is very flammable, and it can be set on fire by the heat from the reaction.

It doesn't matter which metal you use—if it reacts with water, the products are always a metal hydroxide and hydrogen. So, for example, magnesium reacts slowly with water to make magnesium hydroxide and hydrogen. Magnesium hydroxide is used in medicines to cure indigestion.

Rusting

Iron and steel turn rusty in water or damp air. The rust is iron **oxide**, but it forms from iron hydroxide. For rusting to happen, oxygen (usually from the air) and water are needed. Rusting cannot happen if the metal is in contact with only one of these substances. This is why oiling your bicycle chain helps prevent rusting: the oil keeps the water off the steel chain. Paint and plastic coatings also keep the air and water away. Food cans that are made of steel have a coating of tin metal, which does not react with air and water unless it is heated. It stops the steel from rusting and spoiling the food.

Salt speeds up the chemical reactions that cause rusting, so iron and steel rust much more quickly in seawater.

Reactions of metals with acids

You have already seen that some metals react easily with oxygen and water, while others react with difficulty, if at all. It is just the same with the reactions between metals and **acids**.

Salts and hydrogen

When any metal reacts with any acid, the chemical reaction makes a salt and hydrogen gas. For example, here are the equations for the reaction between magnesium and hydrochloric acid:

magnesium + hydrochloric acid → magnesium chloride + hydrogen
$$Mg + 2HCl \rightarrow MgCl_2 + H_2$$

You can tell that a chemical reaction is happening because of the bubbles of hydrogen gas that form. The faster the bubbles form, the faster the reaction. Metals like potassium are so **reactive** that it would be extremely dangerous to add them to an acid. Other metals, like tin and lead, react very slowly with acids, while gold does not react at all.

The right metal for the job

You wouldn't want to use magnesium to make a storage tank for acids, because it would just react with the acid. Although gold does not react with acids, you probably wouldn't choose it to make the storage tank unless you were very wealthy. Lead reacts slowly with hydrochloric acid, but it does not react with sulfuric acid, so it can be used to make storage tanks for sulfuric acid.

 AMAZING FACTS

The pop test

It is easy to test for hydrogen in the laboratory. When you hold a lighted wooden stick over the mouth of a test tube containing the gas, the hydrogen ignites with a popping sound. However, if you have a lot of hydrogen, this can be dangerous.

THE REACTIVITY SERIES

It is possible to list metals in order of their reactivity, from the most reactive at the top, to the least reactive at the bottom. This list is called a **reactivity series**.

Steel food cans have a layer of tin or plastic to stop acidic food like tinned fruit reacting with the iron in the steel. If this layer is damaged, hydrogen gas builds up inside, making the can expand outward.

The Hindenburg was a huge airship, three times longer than a Boeing 747 airliner, which was kept in the air by 262,000 cubic yards (200,000 cubic meters) of hydrogen. When it landed near Lakehurst, New Jersey, in 1937, a spark from static electricity ignited the hydrogen. The airship burst into flames and was destroyed, killing many of the people on-board. Modern airships are lifted by **unreactive** helium instead.

potassium	Most reactive
sodium	
lithium	
calcium	
magnesium	
aluminum	
zinc	
iron	
tin	
lead	
copper	
mercury	
silver	
gold	Least reactive
platinum	

Hydrogen is very flammable and caused this huge fireball that destroyed the airship, the Hindenburg.

Displacement reactions

Metals can push each other around in chemical reactions. More **reactive** metals are able to push out, or displace, less reactive metals from their **compounds**. Chemical reactions where this happens are called **displacement reactions**. So much heat is sometimes produced by these reactions that the metal even melts.

The thermite reaction

How do you join two pieces of railroad track together? You could weld the tracks together by heating the metal so that it melts and joins, but chemistry can come to the rescue, too. The thermite reaction uses a mixture of powdered aluminum and iron **oxide**. When the mixture is ignited, a rapid reaction spreads through it. Aluminum is more reactive than iron, so it displaces iron from iron oxide. In other words, the aluminum "grabs" the oxygen **atoms** off the iron, leaving iron behind. The heat is so intense that the iron melts. The molten iron is run between the tracks where it cools and solidifies, joining the track together. Here are the equations for the thermite reaction:

The **thermite reaction** is a displacement reaction that gives off a lot of heat energy.

aluminum + iron oxide → aluminum oxide + iron

$$2Al + Fe_2O_3 \rightarrow Al_2O_3 + 2Fe$$

Displacement in solution

Displacement reactions also happen when one metal is dissolved to form a solution. This time, though, you don't get flames, smoke, and sparks. Instead, if a more reactive metal is dipped into a solution of a less reactive metal, the less reactive metal coats the surface of the more reactive metal.

For example, iron is more reactive than copper. If you hold an iron nail in some copper chloride solution, the nail quickly gets coated in copper. Here are the equations for this reaction:

iron + copper chloride → iron chloride + copper
$$Fe + CuCl_2 \rightarrow FeCl_2 + Cu$$

One way of looking at the reaction is that iron "grabs" the chlorine atoms off the copper, leaving copper behind. Reactions like these are sometimes called "single displacement" reactions, because only one substance is swapped around, in this case, the chlorine atoms. If you tried to do the reaction the other way around, adding copper to iron chloride, nothing would happen. This is because copper is not reactive enough to displace iron.

CHAPTER 6

Fuels and the environment

Most of the world's supply of energy comes from burning fossil fuels. **Fossil fuels** are coal, crude oil, and natural gas. They are called fossil fuels, because they were made from the remains of living things that died millions of years ago.

Coal

Coal is a black solid that was made from the remains of plants. It sometimes even contains fossilized leaves and bark. During the Carboniferous period, 345–280 million years ago, a lot of the world was covered by swampy forests. It was warmer then, so plants grew very quickly, because the reactions involved in **photosynthesis** could go faster.

When the trees and other plants died, the swampy conditions stopped them from rotting. Instead, they formed layers of dead plants that became squashed by mud and sand. Over thousands of years, chemical reactions warmed the dead plants and turned them into coal. If coal is near the surface, it is scooped out by huge machines, a process called **open-pit mining**, otherwise deep mines are needed.

Most coal is used in power stations to make electricity for lighting and heating, and to run machines.

This is an open-pit coal mine. After the coal has been removed, the soil will be replaced and new trees planted.

Crude oil and natural gas are obtained from deep underground using drilling rigs.

Crude oil and natural gas

Crude oil and natural gas were made from the remains of tiny sea creatures. When these died millions of years ago, they sank to the sea bed. They were covered by mud and sand, and squashed. Over thousands of years, chemical reactions warmed the remains and turned them into oil and gas.

While the oil and gas were forming, the mud and sand on top eventually turned into rock. Water deep underground pushed the oil and gas upward through cracks in the rocks. Sometimes the oil made it all the way up to the surface and tar sands formed. But most of the time, the oil and gas got stuck underneath layers of rocks. That's where it stays until people drill through the rock to reach it.

Fuels, such as gasoline and diesel, come from crude oil. Natural gas is often used for cooking, but it is also used in power stations.

 NONRENEWABLE ENERGY RESOURCES

Fossil fuels are nonrenewable energy resources. They took so long to form, that when we have used them all up, we will never get them back again. They will run out someday. It is estimated that there are 200 years of coal, 40 years of crude oil, and 60 years of natural gas left. More and more, we are using renewable energy resources, such as wind and solar power, to replace fossil fuels, but what about plastics and dyes? Coal and oil are the raw materials for making them. Luckily, chemists can use plants as raw materials instead.

Fuels and burning

Fuels burn when they react with oxygen. Air contains about 21 per cent oxygen, and so air is usually the source of the oxygen needed for burning. The chemical reaction between a fuel and oxygen is called **combustion**. This chemical reaction is also called **oxidation**, because the oxygen **atoms** join to atoms in the fuel to make new substances called **oxides**.

Burning fossil fuels

Coal is almost pure carbon, a shiny black **element**. When carbon burns in plenty of air, the only **product** is carbon dioxide. Here are the equations for the reaction:

carbon + oxygen ➜ carbon dioxide
$$C + O_2 \rightarrow CO_2$$

Crude oil and natural gas are mixtures of **compounds** called **hydrocarbons**. Hydrocarbons are made from just two elements joined together, hydrogen and carbon. There are two products when hydrocarbons burn in plenty of air. These are carbon dioxide and dihydrogen oxide, which is better known as **water**. Here are the equations for the combustion of natural gas (methane):

methane + oxygen ➜ carbon dioxide + water
$$CH_4 + 2O_2 \rightarrow CO_2 + 2H_2O$$

Fossil fuels contain other substances, too. These also react with oxygen during combustion, and some of the products are harmful. You can find out more on pages 40 and 41.

 THE TEST FOR OXYGEN

There is a simple laboratory test to see if oxygen, rather than just air, is in a test tube. When a smoldering wooden stick is put into a test tube of oxygen, it relights.

Evidence for burning

It is usually obvious that something is on fire, because combustion is an exothermic reaction. Energy is released, and you can see flames and feel heat. It is also possible to detect the products of combustion, carbon dioxide, and water. Carbon dioxide makes limewater turn cloudy white (see page 12). Water vapor condenses on cold surfaces as tiny droplets. Water can also be detected using cobalt chloride paper. This is blue when it is dry, but pink when it is damp.

The fire triangle

Combustion needs three things to start or keep going. These are a fuel, heat, and oxygen. If any one of these things is missing, a fire cannot start or keep burning. This is useful to know when you try to put out a fire.

The fire triangle.

 GREAT EXPERIMENTS

Finding oxygen

Until 1641, people thought that air was an element. Then an English scientist named John Mayow experimented with air, mice, and candles. He discovered that the volume of air went down a little when his mice were breathing it or candles were burning in it. Because there was still some gas left when the candles went out, this showed that air contained at least two different gases. Air could not be an element if it contained more than one gas. Another English scientist, Joseph Priestley, discovered oxygen in 1774. He discovered that a gas was given off when he heated mercury oxide. The solid mercury oxide had broken down in the heat to form liquid mercury and oxygen gas.

Air pollution is a serious problem in large, densely-populated cities, such as Mexico City.

Global warming

Carbon dioxide, produced when fossil fuels are burned, is a **greenhouse gas**. This means that it is really good at trapping heat energy in the atmosphere, keeping heat from escaping into space. The amount of fossil fuels being burned has increased greatly since the Industrial Revolution in the nineteenth century. More carbon dioxide is in the atmosphere now than there should be, so more heat is trapped, and the world is warming up. This global warming is changing the weather everywhere. The ice at the Poles is melting and sea levels are rising, leading to flooding.

Dirty smoke

The products of combustion are not completely harmless. When we burn fossil fuels, the substances created can damage the environment. Therefore, we should all try to use only as much energy as we really need. Simply turning off the lights when you leave a room or walking to school instead of going by car helps.

 INCOMPLETE COMBUSTION

Incomplete combustion happens when a fuel burns without a good supply of air. This can happen in engines or when there is not enough ventilation. Instead of carbon dioxide being produced in the reaction, poisonous carbon monoxide is formed. It makes you drowsy and can suffocate you. Carbon monoxide monitors can be installed, which sound an alarm if dangerous amounts of carbon monoxide are present.

Global warming is causing the ice in the Arctic and Antarctic to melt more quickly than it can form.

Global dimming

Amazingly, the amount of sunlight during the daytime is going down around the world. This is called **global dimming**. In the second half of the last century, the amount of daytime sunlight went down by around 10 percent in the United States and United Kingdom. Just like global warming, global dimming is caused by burning fossil fuels. But unlike global warming, which is caused by invisible carbon dioxide gas, it is caused by smoke and soot. These are tiny black particles given off when fuels burn, and they reflect sunlight back into space. Scientists are worried about global dimming. It seems to change the amount of rain falling in some parts of the world, which could make it more difficult to grow crops for food.

 AMAZING FACTS

London's Great Smog of 1952

Smog is a mixture of smoke and fog. It is difficult to see and breathe when there is smog. In 1952, London experienced a particularly bad smog. Fog mixed with smoke from homes and factories that burned coal, making a thick, black smog that lasted for four days. The smog was so thick that people had to guide buses and other vehicles using white rags or flares. Around 4,000 people were killed by it. Nowadays, smokeless fuels make smog like this less likely. Smokeless coal is made by heating coal to drive off the substances that cause smoke and harmful fumes.

Acid rain

Rain is naturally weakly **acidic** because carbon dioxide in the air dissolves in it to make carbonic acid. This is the weak acid that is found in carbonated drinks, which are fizzy because of carbon dioxide bubbles. Unfortunately, the use of fossil fuels makes rain more acidic than normal. This acid rain harms living things and damages buildings.

Sulfur dioxide

Fossil fuels are usually contaminated with small amounts of sulfur. A lot of this can be removed using chemical reactions before the fuel is supplied to customers, but some still remains. When the fuel is burned, the sulfur reacts with oxygen to produce a gas called **sulfur dioxide**. Here are the equations for the reaction:

sulfur + oxygen ➜ sulfur dioxide
$$S + O_2 \rightarrow SO_2$$

Sulfur dioxide has a sharp, choking smell, and it can damage the lungs if it is breathed in. It dissolves in clouds to make sulfurous acid and sulfuric acid, which contribute to acid rain.

Damage to the environment

Acid rain damages rocks and buildings. It weathers limestone and marble, and it **corrodes** metals. Most crop plants do not grow well in acidic soil. When acid rain falls into lakes, the water there becomes too acidic for water plants, and fish and other water animals. These die and the lake becomes lifeless.

NO$_X$

About 79 percent of the air is nitrogen. Usually, this is an **unreactive** gas, but in the heat and pressure of a car engine, it reacts with oxygen. Various nitrogen **oxides** are formed, and together these are called **NO$_X$**. They dissolve in the clouds to form nitrous acid and nitric acid, which also contribute to acid rain.

Trees also die in acid rain, because poisonous aluminum **compounds** are released from the soil and taken up by their roots. So what can be done to prevent all this happening?

Protecting the environment

The extra acid in fields and lakes can be **neutralized** by spreading powdered limestone on them, but it is more difficult to protect buildings and trees. To do this, we have to stop the acidic gases from getting into the air in the first place. The sulfur dioxide from coal-fired power stations is trapped by reacting it with limestone before it leaves the chimneys. The calcium sulfate formed is used to make plasterboard for interior walls.

Acid rain has reacted with this stone statue and weathered its features.

 CATALYTIC CONVERTERS

Catalytic converters are a vital part of modern vehicle exhaust systems. They contain platinum and rhodium, which speed up chemical reactions in the exhaust fumes. These reactions make the exhaust fumes safer. Poisonous carbon monoxide is converted into carbon dioxide, and NO_X (nitrogen oxides) are converted into harmless nitrogen.

Chemistry for the future

It would be easy to think that all the most exciting chemistry discoveries have already been made, but you would be wrong. Chemistry has a great future ahead!

A hydrogen economy

When hydrogen burns, the only product is water, so scientists are very anxious to work out how to use it as an environmentally friendly fuel. Most hydrogen is made at the moment by reacting coal or natural gas with steam. Unfortunately, these are fossil fuels, and so they do not help the problems of global warming and global dimming.

Luckily, hydrogen can be made from water using a chemical reaction called **electrolysis**. This involves passing electricity through the water, which splits it apart into its **elements**, hydrogen and oxygen. The electricity itself can come from wind power, solar power, or another renewable energy resource. Devices called **fuel cells** make electricity using the hydrogen as a fuel. The only waste product is water, and the electricity can be used to power electric motors for cars and buses.

SMART MATERIALS

Have you ever sat on someone's eyeglasses? They probably needed a new pair afterward. However, new smart metals that spring back into shape after being bent have been developed. The metal atoms slip back into their original positions after being moved. Chemists are discovering how to make smart **polymers** that spring back into shape, too. They have even made polymers that conduct electricity and give off light, offering us the possibility of computer screens that can be rolled up like a sheet of paper.

This bus in London uses a hydrogen fuel cell. The only emission from its exhaust is water vapor.

Molecular balls and tubes

Until 1985, chemists thought that carbon only existed in two forms, diamond and graphite. Then a curious **molecule** was discovered with 60 carbon **atoms** joined together like a football. Named **buckminsterfullerene**, it turned out to be just one of many different "fullerenes" made entirely of carbon atoms.

Fullerenes shaped like round cages are called **buckyballs**, and those shaped like incredibly fine tubes are called **nanotubes**. Chemists are investigating the use of buckyballs as lubricants and as tiny medicine capsules, and the use of nanotubes in lightweight, but strong, sports equipment and clothing. It is even possible to trap a molecule of medicine inside the cage of a buckyball, forming a kind of "micropill".

Medicines in the future

Chemists have learned how to react complex mixtures of chemicals to make thousands of substances that might be useful as medicines. They have also discovered that different people respond to medicines in different ways. In the future, we may even get personalized medicines using buckyball molecules to treat our illnesses.

AMAZING FACTS

Living sources of fuel

Researchers at the University of California have produced a strain of tiny **alga** that uses **photosynthesis** to make hydrogen. There is more work to do to make the process efficient enough for commercial use in the future.

Glossary

acid substance with a pH less than 7 that can turn litmus red.

alga a tiny single-celled plant.

alkali soluble base with a pH more than 7 that can turn litmus blue.

alkali metals a group of similar metals including lithium, sodium, and potassium.

atom the small particles from which everything is made.

bases substances that can neutralize acids.

carbonate a compound that contains a carbon atom joined to three oxygen atoms, giving the chemical formula of "CO_3."

cells the small parts that living things are made from.

chloroplasts tiny green objects inside plant cells where photosynthesis happens.

compound substances made from the atoms of two or more elements, chemically joined together.

corrosive able to damage or destroy materials and living tissues.

element substance made from one type of atom.

enzyme substance that speeds up chemical reactions in living things.

fuel cells devices that produce electricity from a fuel, such as hydrogen, and oxygen.

hydrocarbon compound made from hydrogen and carbon only.

hydroxide a compound that contains an oxygen atom and a hydrogen atom joined together, giving a chemical formula with "OH" in it (hydroxides are usually alkalis).

insoluble cannot dissolve in water.

kinetic energy energy contained in all moving things.

microbes living things that can only be seen with a microscope, such as bacteria.

molecule a particle made from two or more atoms chemically joined together.

neutralization chemical reaction in which an acid and a base react together to make a neutral solution.

neutralize to change an acidic or alkaline solution to a neutral solution.

ore substance from which metals can be taken out and purified.

oxidation reaction in which a substance combines with oxygen to make an oxide.

oxide a compound formed when a substance reacts with oxygen is an oxide.

oxidize to react with oxygen.

oxidizer substance that provides oxygen in an oxidation reaction.

pH a measure of how acidic or alkaline a solution is. The pH scale runs from 0 (very acidic) to 14 (very alkaline), with pH 7 meaning neutral.

photosynthesis chemical reaction used by plants to make glucose and oxygen from carbon dioxide and water, using light energy.

polymer large molecules made from smaller molecules joined end to end.

products the substances made in a chemical reaction.

reactants the substances that react together in a chemical reaction.

reactive able to react with another substance easily.

respiration the chemical reaction used by living cells to release energy from glucose.

soluble able to dissolve in water.

unreactive not able to react easily with other substances.

Further information

Books

Energy Essentials: Fossil Fuel, Nigel Saunders and Steven Chapman. Raintree Freestyle, 2004.

Horrible Science: Chemical Chaos, Nick Arnold. Scholastic Hippo, 1997.

Periodic Table Series, Nigel Saunders. Heinemann Library, 2004 and 2005.

Science Files: Chemical Changes, Steve Parker. Heinemann Library, 2002.

Wow Science Series: Chemistry—Flames Are Stored Sunlight, Bryson Gore. Franklin Watts Ltd, 2005.

Web Sites

Due to the changing nature of Internet links, The Rosen Publishing Group, Inc., has developed an online list of Web sites related to the subject of this book. This site is updated regularly. Please use this link to access the list: www.rosenlinks.com/ps/chemical/

Index

48